SPIRIT OF PLACE

PROVENCE

There is the first time we go abroad, and the
first time we go to Provence.

CYRIL CONNOLLY, *ENEMIES OF PROMISE*, 1938

Arcade Publishing
New York

THE SOUTHERN COUNTRY

The southern country flushes to tender spring green only here and there. The cultivated hillsides keep their darker colours, though they may be most sweetly lit with the pink of almonds. March would be a glorious month in Provence if it were only for the almond blossom. Mixed with the soft grey of the olives it makes delicious pictures and it is to be found everywhere. And the wild rosemary is in flower – great bushes of it, lighting up the rocky hillsides with their delicate blue. They were all around me as I sat on this height, and there were brooms getting ready to flower, and wild lavender, and thyme. The air held an aromatic fragrance, and as I walked on between the pines and the deciduous trees, not yet in leaf, the birds were singing and the water rushing down its channels from the snowy heights very musically. There were primroses and violets by the roadside, as if it had been spring in England, and juicy little grape hyacinths to remind one that it was not. There was something to look at and enjoy at every step.

ARCHIBALD MARSHALL, *A SPRING WALK IN PROVENCE*, 1920

A PROVENCAL PATCHWORK

The buckled roofs of orange tiles upon the housetops form indeed one of the most constant and characteristic elements of any tour through the country: the tiled roofs of the backstreets of Avignon, seen from the Papal bedchamber; the rooftops of Vaison shimmering in the heat of June; the rooftops of the port of Martigues, of isolated cabins in the countryside round Aix, of the village of Mallane and the town of Saint-Rémy . . . one's chief memories of a journey through Provence are colour-memories; and I realized this once more as I stood looking down at the Durance and at Sisteron, for the elms, poplars and even the fresh oak-trees along the river's banks showed dark against the startling apple-green of the water-meadows, and the faultless blue of the sky.

JAMES POPE-HENNESSY, ASPECTS OF PROVENCE, 1952

ARLES

The city of Arles is small and packed. A man may spend an hour in it instead of a day or a year, but in that time he can receive full communion with antiquity. For as you walk along the tortuous lanes between high houses, passing on either hand as you go the ornaments of every age, you turn some dirty little corner or other and come suddenly upon the titanic arches of Rome.

HILAIRE BELLOC, *HILLS AND THE SEA*, 1906

MEMORIES OF THE PROVENCE COAST

Early morning on the Mediterranean: bright air resinous with Aleppo pine, water spraying over the gleaming tarmac of the Route Nationale and darkly reflecting the spring-summer green of the planes; swifts wheeling round the oleanders, waiters unpiling the wicker chairs and scrubbing the café tables; armfuls of carnations on the flower-stalls, pyramids of aubergines and lemons, *racasses* on the fishmonger's slab goggling among the wine-dark urchins; smell of brioches from the bakeries, sound of reed curtains jingling in the barber shops, clang of the tin kiosks opening for *Le Petit Var*. Rope-soles warming up on the cobbles by the harbour where the *Jean d'Agrève* prepares for a trip to the Islands and the Annamese boy scrubs her brass. Now cooks from many yachts step ashore with their market-baskets, one-eyed cats scrounge among the fish-heads, while the hot sun refracts the dancing sea-glitter on the café awnings, and the sea becomes a green gin-fizz of stillness in whose depth a quiver of sprats charges and counter-charges in the pleasure of fishes.

CYRIL CONNOLLY, *THE UNQUIET GRAVE*, 1945

THE HILLS OF PROVENCE

We had a most delicious journey to Marselles through a Country, sweetly declining to the South & Mediterranean Coasts, full of Vine-yards, & Olive-yards, Orange trees, Myrtils, Pomegranads & the like sweete Plantations, to which belong innumerable pleasantly situated Villas, to the number of above 15 hundred; built all of Freestone, and most of them in prospect shewing as if they were so many heapes of snow dropp'd out of the clowds amongst the perennial greenes.

JOHN EVELYN, *DIARY*, 7 OCTOBER 1644

'A MINIATURE PROMISED LAND'

I sat down to take my last look at the green valley now lying far beneath me. It showed as a level carpet of vivid green, broken by the grey mass and outlying buildings of the town, with the river threading it lengthwise. The hills rose up sheer on every side. Their lower slopes were so regularly terraced that at this distance they had the effect of horizontal 'shadings' in a pencil drawing. Above that they were grey, and dark green, and red as with heather, and the summits of some of them still held snow. White roads jagged them here and there, but the flat valley floor had the effect of being completely cupped and confined by the rugged heights, as indeed it is, except just where the river, having filled up the bottom of the cup with a layer of rich alluvium, must have broken through at some time, and left the fertile plain all ready and waiting for cultivation. It was like looking down on a miniature Promised Land, so marked was the contrast between the fresh green of the valley and the sombre tones of its encircling hills.

ARCHIBALD MARSHALL, *A SPRING WALK IN PROVENCE*, 1920

MARSEILLES

I was much pleased with Marseilles, which is indeed a noble city, large, populous, and flourishing. The streets, of what is called the new town, are open, airy and spacious; the houses well built, and even magnificent. The harbour is an oval basin, surrounded on every side by the buildings or the land, so that the shipping lies perfectly secure; and here is generally an incredible number of vessels. On the city side, there is a semi-circular quay of free-stone, which extends thirteen-hundred paces; and the space between this and the houses that front it, is continually filled with a surprising crowd of people. . . Marseilles is a gay city, and the inhabitants indulge themselves in a variety of amusements. They have assemblies, a concert spirituel, and a comedy. Here is also a spacious cours, or walk shaded with trees, to which in the evening there is a great resort of well-dressed people.

TOBIAS SMOLLETT, *TRAVELS THROUGH FRANCE AND ITALY*, 10 May 1765

'A GOURMET'S GUIDE'

The best shell-fish are the *praires* and the *clovisses*, about the same size as walnuts or little neck clams; the *clovisses* are the largest, and rather take the place of oysters when the latter is not in season, in the same way the clam does in America; others are mussels, oysters and *langoustes. Langoustes* differ as much as a skinny fowl from a *Poularde de Mans.* Monsieur Echénard [a Marseilles restaurateur] gets his from Corsica, and you then learn how they can vary. He has also a *Poularde Réservé en Cocotte Raviolis*, which is a dish to be remembered; and a small fat sole caught between Hyères and Toulon is not to be despised.

NATHANIEL NEWNHAM-DAVIS & ALGERNON BASTARD, *A GOURMET'S GUIDE TO EUROPE*, 1903

CAP CANAILLE

Eastward from Cassis we cross the neck of the promontory which ends as Cap Canaille and the Bec d'Aigle. We leave the cape to our right, and soon lose the view of the carpet of scrub, its ilexes and its scented bush of rosemary and wild marjoram. We zigzag down to La Ciotat. It is quite a large place of more than ten thousand inhabitants spread along a bay five miles wide and closed southwards by the imposing and monumental Bec d'Aigle or Eagle's Beak, which is separated by a channel from the Ile Verte. It is from this island that you get the best view of the Eagle's Beak cleaving the waters like the prow of a great ship and a landmark for all this southern shore.

ALAN HOUGHTON BRODERICK, *PROVENCE AND THE RIVIERA*, 1952

MONT SAINTE-VICTOIRE

It is nearly 4 o'clock, there is no air at all. The weather is still stifling. I am waiting for the moment when the carriage will take me to the river. I spend some pleasant hours there. There are some large trees that form a vault over the water. I am going to a spot known as *Gour de Martelly*, which is on the little '*chemin des Milles*' that leads to Montbriant. Towards the evening cows come which are being brought there to pasture. There is plenty of material to study and make masses of pictures.

PAUL CEZANNE, LETTER TO HIS SON, PAUL, 2 SEPTEMBER 1906

One day I set out to walk to the next village to Le Tholonet, Beaurecueil... Along the roadside, and in the fields below the level of the road, were flowers: a profusion of wild gladioli in a stream-bed, dark blue and bright yellow flowers, and everywhere grey bushes of wild lavender. The earth was the colour of rust... I sat on a large rock beside the road to study carefully the constant brooding companion of this and all other walks one could take in that direction – Mont Sainte-Victoire. From Aix and Tholonet this celebrated mountain had looked compact and high; as one walked toward Beaurecueil it appeared to unfurl, or to unfold like a screen, revealing itself as a long range rather than a mountain, and seeming somehow biscuit-thin.

JAMES POPE-HENNESSY, *ASPECTS OF PROVENCE*, 1952

AIX-EN-PROVENCE

So we went on, until eleven at night, when we halted at the town of Aix (within two stages of Marseilles) to sleep.

The hotel, with all the blinds and shutters closed to keep the light and heat out, was comfortable and airy next morning, and the town was very clean; but so hot, and so intensely light, that when I walked out at noon it was like coming suddenly from the darkened room into crisp blue fire. The air was so very clear, that distant hills and rocky points appeared within an hour's walk: while the town immediately at hand – with a kind of blue wind between me and it – seemed to be white hot, and to be throwing off a fiery air from its surface.

CHARLES DICKENS, *PICTURES FROM ITALY*, 1846

A.E.WAITE

'TEMPLE AND ALTAR'

There is no untidiness, no harshness, nothing that jars; nor is there any hint of weakness about the smooth, bold contours, rising towards the sun, of Mount Olympus of Trets and Mont Sainte-Victoire. These are the façade of the distant mountain ranges of the Etoile and the Sainte-Baume. Sainte-Victoire is the heart of the Aix countryside, its temple and altar, its spirit and substance. Transparent and ethereal, vibrating with life at daybreak, kindled to fire at sunset, cloud-capped majestically in stormy weather – it is a soul made visible, a living force that reflects every change in weather or season. It casts a veritable spell over the countryside that it enobles and cheers all who see it.

JOSEPH D'ARBAUD, *LA PROVENCE*, 1939

THE ROAD TO ST TROPEZ

We crossed the mountains, and wandered by crooked unknown paths, and beds of torrents, and then found the village of Gassing [Gassin] on the top of a mountain, which, however, was more than a league from that to which we intended to go. . . I breakfasted on grapes, rye bread and bad wine. Mules were reported to abound in this village, or rather that which we missed; but the master of the only two we could hear of being absent, I had no other resource, than agreeing with a man to take my baggage on an ass, and myself to walk a league further, to San Tropes, for which he demanded 3 liv. In two hours reached that town, which is prettily situated, and tolerably well built, on the banks of a noble islet of the sea. From Cavalero [Cavalaire] hither, the country is all mountain, eighteen-twentieths of it covered with pines, or a poor wilderness of evergreen shrubs, rocky and miserable. . . The whole coast of Provence is nearly the same desert; yet the climate would give, on all these mountains, productions valuable for feeding sheep and cattle; but they are incumbered with shrubs absolutely worthless.

ARTHUR YOUNG, *TRAVELS IN FRANCE*, 1792

'THE GREAT WINES OF THE SOUTH . . .

Meanwhile . . . the familiar prospects of vines, olives, cypresses; one comes to believe that they are Platonic abstractions rooted in the imagination of man. Symbols of the Mediterranean, they are always there to welcome one – either trussed back by the winter gales in glittering silver-green bundles, or softly powdered by the gold dust of the summers, blown from the threshing floors by the freshets of sea-wind. Yet, the great wines of the south sleep softly on the French earth like a pledge that the enchanted landscapes of the European heart will always exist, will never fade against this taut wind-haunted blue sky where the mistral rumbles and screams all winter long.

LAWRENCE DURRELL, 'RIPE LIVING IN PROVENCE', IN *HOLIDAY*, 1959

AUTUMN IN PROVENCE

On a clear October morning, when the vineyards are taking their last tints of gold and crimson, and the yellow foliage of the poplars by the river mingles with the sober greys of olive-trees and willows, every square inch of this landscape, glittering as it does with light and with colour, the more beautiful for its subtlety and rarity, would make a picture.

JOHN ADDINGTON SYMONDS, *SKETCHES AND STUDIES IN ITALY*, 1879

THE BLUE BAY

Chance led me one autumn to a secluded nook on the Côte d'Azur, between Marseilles and Toulon, and there I fell in with one or two painters who revelled in the methods of the modern French school.

Winston Churchill, Painting as a Pastime, 1948

To look at it from the outside, the Cap d'Antibes is just a long low spit of dull olive-grey land, but, within, it has sea and mountain views most gloriously beautiful. To the east you see everything you can see from Nice, to the west you see everything you can see from Cannes; to the north, a gigantic range of snow-covered Alps; to the south, and all around, the sky-blue Mediterranean. For the Cape is a promontory made up of lots of little promontories, each jutting into the sea at all possible angles, and with endless miniature bays, mimic islets, their white rocks jagged and worn by the dashing waves, that break over them in ceaseless spray, even in glassy weather. To sit among oranges, olives, and palms, as at Algiers or Palermo, and yet look up from one's seat under one's vine and fig-tree, to see the snow-clad Alps glowing pink in the sunset as at Zermatt or Chamonix, is a combination of incongruous delights nowhere else to be met in Europe.

Augustus Hare, The Rivieras, 1896

ANTIBES

Our Antibes is charming! a harbour, a mole, a lighthouse, everything as at Bigorneau, but a little larger; pleasant ramparts just high enough to give a lovely view to the people who there take their daily constitutional.

The little lighthouse is so small that it hardly lights anything but itself; the little mole only embraces just so much sea as so little a town could feel inclined for; the little harbour only receives a few tartanes, now and then a coasting brig called always by the Provençeaux a 'brigoulette'. . . The tartanes are 'like painted ships on a painted ocean', over their reflections. A boat comes in; all awakes; hulls dance, masts bob and curtsey, and their lengthened reflection goes curling and twisting in the clear water with a red flame at the end . . . and everywhere something lovable and tender, made more tender by the contrast of deep sky, great sea, immeasurable Alps, and of Nice, of which one has a glimpse over there, between Alps and sea, a long line of white houses in a mist of silver.

PAUL ARENE, IN E. I. ROBSON, *A WAYFARER IN PROVENCE*, 1926

APPROACHING GRASSE

As we approached Grasse, the colour of the leaves on the olive trees took a deeper green; the trees themselves were as large as willows. The fig trees are often eight inches around the trunk, exactly like the trees on the road to Portici. That is because Grasse is sheltered from the north by a mountain that is bare on top. At last I have seen rose bushes cultivated in the open. The wind was from the south and rolling up enormous clouds; I fear we shall have rain.

Suddenly I saw Grasse, flat against a little hill and surrounded by other hills covered with olive trees that looked as though they were about to hurl themselves down on the town. . . On arriving in Grasse, we found a terrace filled with great trees, far more beautiful than the trees of Saint-Germain. On the right and on the left, mountains literally covered to their summits with tufted olive trees and, down below, a vast expanse of sea which, as the crow flies, does not seem to be more than two miles away.

STENDHAL (HENRI BEYLE), *TRAVELS IN THE SOUTH OF FRANCE*, 1833

A POET IN PROVENCE

I wander aimlessly from lane to lane,
bending a careful ear to ancient times:
the same cicadas sang in Caesar's reign,
upon the walls the same sun clings and climbs.

The plane tree sings: with light its trunk is pied;
the little shop sings: delicately tings
the bead-stringed curtain that you push aside –
and, pulling on his thread, the tailor sings.

And at a fountain with rounded rim,
rinsing blue linen, sings a village girl,
and mottle shadows of the plane tree swim
over the stone, the wickerwork, and her.

What bliss it is, in this world of song,
to brush against the chalk of walls, what bliss
to be a Russian poet lost among
cicadas trilling with a Latin lisp.

VLADIMIR NABOKOV, 'PROVENCE', 1923

RENOIR AT CAGNES

In my father's day Cagnes was a thriving village of prosperous peasants. . . My father felt at home with them. They showed little or no curiosity about his painting; and he, for his part, was content to congratulate them when they had had a good harvest. The local products were varied. The wine from certain hillsides had a sharp flavour, but was excellent; and the Neapolitan fishermen at Cross-de-Cagnes brought in their nets filled with little silvery sardines, which my father said were the best in the world. Their wives carried them in flat baskets, which they balanced on their heads, calling in a raucous voice, 'Au pei! Au pei!' ('Fresh fish! Fresh fish!') to attract customers. Some of them posed for Renoir.

What pleased him particularly at Cagnes was that you did not have your nose 'right up against the mountains'. He was fond of mountains, but at a distance. 'They should remain what God created them for: a background, as in Giorgione.' He often said to me that he knew nothing in the world more beautiful than the valley of the Cagnes river, when you can just make out the Baou mountain at Saint-Jeanet through the reeds which give the river its name. Cagnes seemed to be waiting for Renoir, and he adopted it, as one gives oneself to a girl of whom one has dreamt all one's life and then discovered on the doorstep after having roamed the world over.

Jean Renoir, Renoir, My Father, 1962

THE LEGEND OF THE GOLDEN GOAT

So popular has the goat been in Provence that there are innumerable legends and stories about it, the favourite of which is certainly the tale of the Golden Goat. Alphonse Daudet, Paul Arène and Frederic Mistral have all written about him. All believe to have seen him in different parts of the country. An old peasant of the Camargue told me his story and insisted that those who said his favourite home was near Les Baux or in the sacred forest of La Sainte-Baume were quite wrong. 'Of course I know, Madame,' he said, 'that the Golden Goat roves all over the whole country, but his real home is in the Camargue. On moonlight nights one can hear his hoofs rapping on the roads; sometimes one sees him grazing among the rocks. But it is not a good omen for anyone but a Provençal to see him. He belongs to *us* and will do none of us any harm, but others may not look at him when he is doing his work. . . The Golden Goat goes from place to place to take care of the treasures of the country. If he finds someone spoiling them he butts them with his horns and they are immediately bewitched.'

ELEANOR ELSNER, *ROMANTIC FRANCE*, 1926

A POSTCARD FROM PROVENCE

Yesterday was about the most lovely in my life. Started out on motor scooter along famous wide 'promenade des anglais' of Nice, with its out-door cafés, splendid baroque façades, rows of palms, strolling musicians – and headed inland to Vence, where I planned to see the beautiful recent Matisse cathedral of my art magazine, which I've loved via pictures for years.

How can I describe the beauty of the country? Everything is so small, close, exquisite and fertile. Terraced gardens on steep slopes of rich, red earth, orange and lemon trees, olive orchards, tiny pink and peach houses. To Vence – small, on a sun-warmed hill, uncommercial, slow, peaceful. Walked to Matisse cathedral – small, pure, clean-cut. White, with a blue-tile roof sparkling in the sun. But shut! Only open to public two days a week. A kindly talkative peasant told me stories of how rich people came daily in large cars from Italy, Germany, Sweden, etc., and were not admitted, even for large sums of money. I was desolate and wandered to the back of the walled nunnery, where I could see a corner of the garden and sketched it, feeling like Alice outside the garden, watching the white doves and orange trees. Then I went back to the front and stared with my face through the barred gate. I began to cry. I knew it was so lovely inside, pure white with the sun through blue, yellow, and green stained windows.

Then I heard a voice, "Ne pleurez, entrez," and the Mother Superior let me in, after denying all the wealthy people in cars.

I just knelt in the heart of the sun and the colors of sky, sea, and sun, in the pure white heart of the Chapel. "Vous êtes si gentille," I stammered. The nun smiled. "C'est la miséricorde de Dieu." It was.

SYLVIA PLATH, POSTCARD TO HER MOTHER, 7 JANUARY 1956

THE CÔTE D'AZUR

Echoes of former glories persist along the now comparatively shabby haunts of the Côte d'Azur. . .

In Nice the Hotel Negresco with its wedding-cake façade, though slightly cracked, is still like icing sugar in the sun. But the vestibule is almost empty. The Promenade des Anglais is sparsely populated with a few old cronies. The reaper has taken his toll, and economics as well as fashions have brought this sad change. . .

Even before the last war, the seasons switched and the popularity of the Riviera was confined to the months of summer. The dangerous, curving Corniche road was jammed with sports cars on the way from one *plage* to another; sunbathing ladies covered in Ambre Solaire, rich young girls and boys, all dressed as sailors, brought millions of francs and pounds and dollars to the new owners of casinos and night-clubs. The old winter châteaux were ill-suited to conversion to summer usage, but small gardeners' lodges, or servants' quarters, were decorated by Lady Mendl, and once more the Riviera was rich.

CECIL BEATON, *DIARY*, JANUARY 1955

CARNIVAL AT NICE

Carnival at Nice begins with a great procession, and every one turns out to meet King Carnival with all sorts of illuminations, noise of trumpets, dancing and singing. It would seem as if the entire population had taken leave of its senses. The procession will come to an end about half-past ten, but the dancing and jollifications are prolonged for some hours afterwards. In these modern days with all sorts of facilities of lights and other properties unknown to those of ancient days, the procession can be carried out with a very considerable amount of magnificence. There are, of course, many bands, both in the procession itself and in the Place Masséna. The progress or procession goes on two or three different times, and there is a final parade on Shrove Tuesday, when King Carnival, amid the glory of fireworks, is burned in effigy.

E. I. ROBSON, *A WAYFARER IN PROVENCE*, 1926

THE VIEW FROM NICE

When I stand on the rampart and look around me, I can scarce help thinking myself inchanted. The small extent of country which I see, is all cultivated like a garden. Indeed, the plain presents nothing but gardens, full of green trees, loaded with oranges, lemons, citrons and bergamots, which make a delightful appearance. If you examine them more nearly, you will find plantations of green pease ready to gather; all sorts of sallading, and pot-herbs, in perfection; and plats of roses, carnations, ranunculas, anemonies, and daffodils, blowing in full glory, and with such beauty, vigour, and perfume, as no flower in England ever exhibited.

TOBIAS SMOLLETT, *TRAVELS THROUGH FRANCE AND ITALY*, 1766

'THE LAST SIGH OF FRANCE . . .'

Now only the *commune* of Menton lies before the Italian border; Menton, the last sigh of France, a mellowed place like an old theatre curtain, charming and slow, a suntrap where bananas and lemons grow. The Royal Westminster Hotel, dark-panelled, might have moved from Victorian Scotland overnight; yet has a tropical garden . . . and lies beneath the old Italian town whose glory is a finely paved square set between two baroque churches, where now every year a festival of chamber music is held by the light of oil lanterns and the star-studded Italian sky, fragile and brilliant music bounded by stone architectures and the night.

WILLIAM SANSOM, *BLUE SKIES, BROWN STUDIES*, 1953

ACKNOWLEDGEMENTS

PICTURE CREDITS

Front cover: *Paysage en été*, Pierre Auguste Renoir (Fine Art Photographic Library)
Back cover: *Landscape*, Alfred Renaudin (Bridgeman Art Library)
Frontispiece: *Village sur la Côte*, Lucien Pissarro (Christie's Colour Library)
2: *Lavender field*, Dennis Stock (Magnum)
3: *Village and olive groves*, Dennis Stock (Magnum)
5: *Village de Provence*, André Derain (Christie's)
6: *Arles*, Horst Munzig (Susan Griggs Agency)
7: *Les Alicamps at Arles*, Frank Randal (Bridgeman/Victoria & Albert Museum)
9: *Paysage en été*, Pierre Auguste Renoir (Fine Art Photographic)
11: *Brantes, below Mt Ventoux*, Charlie Waite (Landscape Only)
13: *A French Village*, Paul Guigou (Fine Art Photographic)
15: *Marseilles*, Richard Kalvar (Magnum)
17: *Fish market in Marseilles*, Henri Cartier-Bresson (Magnum/John Hillelson Agency)
19: *Cap Canaille, above Cassis*, Charlie Waite (Landscape Only)
21: *Mont Ste-Victoire*, Paul Cézanne (Metropolitan Museum of Art New York)
23: *Aix-en-Provence: The Fountain*, Alexander Waite (Bridgeman)
25: *Mt Ste-Victoire*, John Heseltine (Susan Griggs Agency)
27: *St-Tropez – vu du jardin de l'Hôtel Latitude*, Henri Manguin (Christie's)
29: *Vineyard near La Cadière*, Patrick Eagar
31: *Vineyard near Aubagne*, Charlie Waite (Landscape Only)
33: *The Blue Bay*, Sir John Lavery (Bridgeman/Spink & Son)
35: *Antibes*, Claude Monet (Toledo Museum of Art, Toledo, Ohio – Gift of Edward Drummond Libbey)
37: *Grasse*, Thomas Austin Brown (Bridgeman/V&A Museum)

39: *Provençal street scene*, Dennis Stock (Magnum)
41: *View of Cagnes*, Pierre Auguste Renoir (Bridgeman/Saarland Museum Saarbrucken)
43: *Provençal goatherd*, Guy Le Querrec (Magnum)
45: *Landscape*, Dennis Stock (Magnum)
47: *Elegante au bord de la mer*, François Flameng (Bridgeman/Whitford & Hughes)
49: *Mardi Gras in Nice*, Carl Purcell (Image Bank)
51: *Terrace at Nice*, John Fulleylove (Bridgeman/V&A Museum)
53: *Place à Menton*, Jean François Raffaelli (Fine Art Photographic)
55: *Sunflower crop*, Tony Stone

TEXT CREDITS

Text extracts from the following sources are reprinted with the kind permission of the publishers and copyright holders stated. Should any copyright holder have been inadvertently omitted they should apply to the publishers who will be pleased to credit them in full in any subsequent editions.

Page 6: Hilaire Belloc, *Hills and the Sea* (Methuen, 1906); 4, 20: James Pope-Hennessy, *Aspects of Provence* (Longman, 1952/Penguin Books); 8: Cyril Connolly, *The Unquiet Grave* (Hamish Hamilton, 1945); 18: Alan Houghton Broderick, *Provence and the Riviera* (Hodder & Stoughton, 1952); 28: Laurence Durrell, *Spirit of Place* (Faber & Faber, 1969); 38: Vladimir Nabokov, 'Provence' (1923) in *Poems and Problems* (Weidenfeld & Nicolson, 1973/Smith/Skolnik, New York); 40: Jean Renoir, *Renoir, My Father* (Collins, 1962/A.D. Peters & Co. Ltd); 44: Sylvia Plath, *Letters Home* (Faber & Faber, 1975); 46: Cecil Beaton *The Restless Years: Diaries 1955-63* (Weidenfeld & Nicolson, 1976); 52: William Sansom, *Blue Skies Brown Studies* (Hogarth Press, 1953).

Published in the United States by Arcade Publishing, Inc.,
a Little, Brown company.

Library of Congress Cataloging-in-Publication Data is available.

ISBN 1-55970-007-6
First American Edition

Conceived, edited and designed by Russell Ash and Bernard Higton
Printed and bound in Spain by Cayfosa, Barcelona

10 9 8 7 6 5 4 3 2 1